Ukraine Rising

by

Ido Graf

I dedicate this novel to:

All the innocents, and especially the children, who suffer and die during time of war.

'Omnia Vincit Amor et nos cedamus amori.'

'Love conquers all; let us all yield to love.'

Bucolica or Eclogae Publius 37 B.C,
Vergilius Maro (Vergil).

Also, by Ido Graf

In the Adam Wolf series:

'Eye Kill'
'See Glass' – Repeated **Amazon Best Seller** in Multiple Categories, Internationally.

Short Stories:

'Ukraine Rising'

Media Requests & Film Rights

All press enquiries or film rights requests relating to Ido Graf's books should be directed to his publicist.

Any negotiations regarding the novels should be directed to his lawyers of choice in Washington D.C.

Please make any enquiries through the contact page.

https://www.idograf.com

ISBN: 978-1-9162140-7-1

Contents

Prologue
On the road from Kyiv to Bucha,
Kyiv Oblast, Ukraine

Amy could sense beads of sweat forming across her brow and her upper lip. It was stiflingly hot in the back of the battered old Lada and yet, oddly enough, it smelt of damp. The car did not benefit from air conditioning nor much else, she thought.

She yearned for the comparative comfort of the taxis in her home city of Chicago, which she had left behind a week before. If Amy had only known, she was lucky to get the vehicle as the country was short on stock since the war.

The young freelance journalist had run her window down to try to relieve her discomfort. She couldn't help but wonder if the warm air which streamed in made matters worse. Eventually Amy decided to put the window back up, but as she turned the handle it came away in her hand. Stifling a laugh, the journalist looked furtively towards the driver and then quietly placed it in the footwell. As Amy set it down, she wondered how something that felt so solid could come away so easily with little pressure.

Ever since she had left the capital, Kyiv, Amy had noticed the incredibly beautiful roadside embankments. They were all alive with the most beautiful multi-coloured wildflowers and berry-laden trees which happily danced in the light wind. They continually filled the car with the most glorious and intoxicating scents. She was captivated by the ranks of colour as the petals danced in any passing breeze.

Being very environmentally aware the journalist had never much liked roads or the vehicles which used them. She had steadfastly refused to get a driving license, though she did bend her own rules by taking taxis and lifts from friends.

'A girl has to have some vices after all!' She thought.

While she sat in the back seat, she pondered the highways of Ukraine and sensed that they could almost change her view. Amy had come to the country in the hope that she would find inspiration for a news story which might make her name.

She commented to the driver on how lucky his people were to have such beauty in their countryside, and which often extended into the cities. The journalist thought it odd that, though he had been very talkative up to that point, he suddenly went quiet and had, what appeared to be, a sullen look written across his face.

Amy bounced the idea around in her head as she gently tried to brush the folds out of her dress with a firm flat hand. She considered, '...maybe I could call the article 'Flower Power – The Power of Change!'

Amy smiled to herself and laughed it off. 'No! I need to find something more 'highbrow.'

She had noticed, some time before, that the traffic was getting heavier. Then, it lightened up as the newly constructed addition to the road became two lanes. But it was bizarre. Amy noted that most of the traffic had moved over to the lane which bordered the grass verge and that the vehicles had become even more slow-moving. As Amy's vehicle drove past, she noticed cars parked up haphazardly on the road, the grass embankment and on into neighbouring fields.

The journalist, her interest aroused, asked the taxi driver, 'What are all these people doing?'

The man looked at her in the rear-view mirror, saying slowly and cryptically, 'Maybe it is better that I show you, 'as' I tell you!'

She was surprised and intrigued.

He pulled the taxi over, squeezing off the road between two particularly, badly parked cars. One of them still had what looked like shrapnel damage along the side.

As they both climbed out of the vehicle, they could see a long line of people queuing quietly. They had been partly obscured by the parked vehicles and because the land slipped away into a valley below. Amy was also more aware of the overpowering and wonderful scents of the flowers which filled the air. They patiently waited a long way ahead of a large group of others who were gathered silently around something – but Amy knew not what. The writer noticed that all the people looked respectful, many seemed to be praying and most carried small linen packets and flowers.

Fascinated, Amy turned to the driver with a questioning look on her face. She was surprised to see that he looked sad. Stepan gave her a gentle smile and then began to recount his story.

Chapter One
Suburbs, Saint Petersburg, Russian Federation

Near the outskirts of Saint Petersburg an elderly woman knelt by a beautifully, manicured grave. Irina had a small, cheap hand broom which she used to brush the dust away carefully and methodically from the headstone. As she did so, she chatted to Viktor about their son and her fears for him. Viktor had died ten years before in an accident at the factory where he had worked. Irina received no compensation and her life had become increasingly difficult since his loss. She had done her best to look after their young son, making what money she could with multiple part-time jobs. The boy, Konstantin, had joined the army once he reached eighteen. He was an intelligent, sensitive, kindly soul who should, by all rights, have gone on to further his studies. However, he desperately wanted to help his mother and he had been told by the recruiters that he would make a good living in the army and that he would learn many skills. They had lied on both counts.

Some months later the Russian government decided to invade Ukraine, once again, and Konstantin was horrified to find that he was at war.

A bitter wind began to blow, and Irina pulled her thin woollen coat close to her. She stood up uneasily, said her goodbyes to Viktor, and slowly walked the mile or so to the Orthodox Church which she regularly attended. Outside the Church, on the steps an old man sat huddled against a wall. He looked barely alive and even colder than she felt. Irina fumbled in her pocket and pulled out the few coins that were there. She looked longingly at the money and then dropped half of it into the small tin that sat to the side of the beggar. As the coins hit the metal base, they made a dull hollow sound. But to the destitute man it was a sound more pleasurable than any score by the city's famous and former resident, Tchaikovsky. Then Irina slowly walked into the church. The old man thanked her effusively as she quietly disappeared.

The Church was dark and opulent and there was an overpowering smell of incense which permeated everything. The building was empty, and she found it so completely comforting. Irina walked over to a nook where rows of candles were supported in ornate metal holders. Dropping the last of her coins into a small box,

Irina then lit her own candle. Feeling exhausted, Irina staggered over to the wooden pew and then the kindly old woman knelt down to pray for Viktor and for Konstantin

The decrepit beggar smiled at Irina as he saw her leave the church and his heart lifted to think of her generosity towards him. She was dirt poor but, despite or because of that, she remained good and kind.

Chapter Two
On the road from Odessa to Uman, Cherkasy Oblast, central Ukraine

The small platoon from the 3rd Company of the Ukrainian Naval Infantry Corps were far from their normal operating areas along the coast. But much had been in flux since the start of the Russian invasion. Men and materials were drawn desperately from everywhere to defend against the onslaught.

The resilience within the country and its people was being tested to the limit.

The Ukrainian Marines were some of the bravest and most highly trained of the Ukrainian forces, which said a great deal. The men of the platoon were pushing themselves hard. They had marched, cycled, taken lifts in cars from a willing population and had eventually hitched rides on tanks to head as fast as they could towards the frontline and on to Bucha. There had been rumours of atrocities and several of the men in the platoon had families from that region. The soldiers had been unable to contact their relatives since the war had begun.

It was a stressful and difficult time for the Marines, but nobody complained. All were lost in their own thoughts. All were single minded!

Chapter Three
Forest, Kyiv Oblast, north-west of Kyiv, Ukraine

Far, far ahead of the Marines, a Russian infantry platoon had begun to realise that things were beginning to go wrong with their army's advance. The men were blindly unaware as to how badly.

Their radio operator had been killed when he had inadvertently stood on a mine. The radio itself was beyond repair which was all that bothered their brutal Corporal. The Russians were crossing through forests heading towards a major road that would lead on to Kyiv. There they hoped to pick up the main column of the Russian advance. There they hoped to reach safety – none, more so than their vicious NCO.

Each of the men kept one eye on the route and one wary eye on their Corporal, Koslov. His skin was sallow from years of drinking vodka, and he had a mean set to his eyes and mouth. He stank of stale smoke and fear.

The NCO had a propensity to violence coupled with a heavy dose of malice.

His men, if you could call them that, would just as easily kill him before they ever killed a Ukrainian. The trick, however, as they all knew, would be getting away with it. So, they marched on in a sullen silence.

Chapter Four
The road from Kyiv to Bucha, Kyiv Oblast, Ukraine

The roads were mostly clear as many of the people who had tried to escape the Russian advance had already made their way to comparative safety. Some had gone to friends and relatives in other more distant areas of Ukraine. Others still had travelled abroad to the many countries who had opened their borders to them, giving them sanctuary. The incredible generosity of their neighbours, both near and far, had deeply touched the Ukrainian people and had left their military better able to concentrate on the task at hand.

There was a constant smell in the air of burning rubber and fuel and the horizon was filled with pockets of dark clouds and occasional explosions. The chatter of birds had all but disappeared from the land. Most of the traffic that remained was military, though the soldiers had to progress with extreme caution as it was not always easy to tell friend from foe. The front was very fluid in those early days.

The Marines sensed a constant danger from harassing enemy helicopters and aeroplanes, though this diminished rapidly as the Russians losses mounted.

Passing Kyiv, and the deeper the Marines got into the Kyiv Oblast, the more they heard of the atrocities that had occurred in and around the city of Bucha. More frequently they began to hear of them first-hand. The horror which they believed lay ahead made them more frantic and they became even more driven.

Before the war many of the men had friends who were Russian or even had family ties to Russia. Some had even worked there in times past. But any sense of camaraderie had long since gone, only to be replaced by something much uglier.

Chapter Five
Open countryside, south of Bucha, Kyiv Oblast, Ukraine

A mother, Kristina, and her two children had managed to hide when the Russians had arrived in Bucha. They eventually made it to the outskirts under cover of the night and then passed on across country heading south. They kept away from the roads for safety. Kristina's children knew that something was wrong even though she had tried to dress their flight up as an adventure.

Before she left, Kristina had seen the bodies of neighbours and friends who had been shot by the invading troops. Some had their hands tied behind their backs and none were soldiers. She had even seen a man on a pedal bike mown down as he cycled home. It had left her terrified and desperate to flee.

As the morning came and having walked all night, the mother felt some relief. The acrid smell of burning was still all around her, as were the sounds of gunfire and explosions but they seemed to be getting more distant.

They had seen a Russian column at one point. Coming to a ridge they looked far below at the long line of vehicles. They were in disarray. Some remained on the road while others were half pulled off it. Plumes of smoke rose from many of the vehicles and there was widespread panic among the troops who had ridden with them. They still appeared to be under attack.

Occasionally a shell in one of the tanks would explode creating even more confusion and fear. The young mother could see that many of the personnel had been killed or wounded and others were retreating in disarray, leaving their comrades to their fate. The tanks at the front and back of the column had been destroyed and this had blocked the rest of the vehicles from moving freely. In the valley floor the ground was boggy and any vehicles which had tried to escape soon became stuck in the mud. The open hatches and doors of many of the trucks and tanks were a testament to their crew's rapid exit when they realised that they were sitting ducks.

Kristina noted that some of the troops, in their flight, were heading in her direction and she quickly altered course to avoid them. However, by doing so she had inadvertently headed towards other dangers.

Chapter Six
Bomb crater, south-east of Bucha, Kyiv Oblast, Ukraine

Off to the east of the young family, huddled in a bomb crater, a young Russian sheltered under a tarpaulin. The driving rain felt intensely cold only exacerbating his sense of despair. As he hid, so he penned a letter to his mother at home, in far off Saint Petersburg. Konstantin tried to write her words of encouragement and to give his beloved mother the sense that he was safe. He was her only child, and they had no other relatives left to speak of. The young man knew that she would be scared for him. He was scared for himself! The carnage and the atrocities that he had witnessed each day were truly horrifying.

Becoming lost in his thoughts, he considered how deeply he regretted having joined the armed forces. He was shocked by the way his fellow soldiers had treated the civilian population and their cruelty, even to children. He had done what he could to try to help and protect those he came across, but it was impossible.

But the cruelty did not end there. The Russian officers and NCOs brutalised their own men too. Sometimes purely for fun and often to force them onwards, to fight in a war most of them did not want. He had been shocked to see two soldiers suddenly shot for refusing to fight. They were not charged and there was no legal process followed and there had been no talk of sending them back to prison in Russia, No! They were just expendable.

The officers and NCOs at his barracks outside of Moscow had been buoyant before the invasion and had boasted that they would be in Kyiv imminently. Within days of the invasion many of those same men were dead and the few who remained did not dare speak to the soldiers of a swift victory. The lie was written bold across the swarms of Russian dead and the swathes of destroyed vehicles.

The rain began to lighten, and Konstantin started to write again. Soon afterwards he heard heavy footsteps approaching and his heart began to sink.

The tarpaulin was roughly pulled from him and standing before him Corporal Koslov screamed in derision, 'Writing to Mummy again Orlov!'

Koslov then stuck his boot firmly into Konstantin's

chest before ripping the letter from his hand as he did so. The thug ripped it to shreds and screamed at all the soldiers, 'Get up we are heading out.'

The young private could smell the stench of alcohol emanating from the Corporal's filthy clothing and assaulting Konstantin's senses. The other infantrymen had watched what had happened to Konstantin. Some sneered at him, enjoying the spectacle of someone else suffering, but all were nervous in case Koslov singled them out next.

They all stood up quickly and made themselves ready.

Koslov was a thuggish brute, but 'he' was also scared. The Corporal knew, all too well, what atrocities his army and he had committed. He also knew that things were going very badly with the advance. He was terrified in case he fell into Ukrainian hands, as he knew that they would not be forgiving once they knew the true nature and scale of what had been done to their innocent families.

He cared nothing for his men. Kozlov's only concern for them, was a selfish one. He would stay with them for as long as they could help to protect him.

The infantrymen were damp and despondent as they headed off. Konstantin, saddened, looked back at the torn letter as it was stamped into the muddy ground by the passing troops.

The pain in his chest from the violent kick felt as if he had been left with one or more cracked ribs.

Suddenly he felt the butt of Kozlov's rifle being slammed, hard, into his helmet followed by a violent push from the brutish Corporal, 'Get going Orlov before I stick some lead into you!'

Koslov remained safely at the back of the line of troops. He remembered the day before when he had lost his radio operator and the man's equipment which had been destroyed. Koslov cursed his luck and the fool who had stepped on the mine. The Corporal walked on without any knowledge of where his main force was and more concerningly where the Ukrainians were.

Watching the soldiers ahead of him and following their tracks he smiled happily to himself thinking that if there were further mines, then his men would die and not he.

Chapter Seven
Open countryside, south-east of Bucha, Kyiv Oblast, Ukraine

Kristina had left her home with a small bag of provisions and two bottles of water. She had rationed them because she dared not go near any villages or towns for further provisions. The young mother was very fatigued and desperate. Occasionally she would stop to allow the children to pick wildflowers or to sit and rest. While the little ones played the woman would listen furtively to her radio for information about the war and the Russian advance. Her phone had stopped working soon after the attack and it lay in her bag empty of charge.

Occasionally she would watch the little ones happily playing with each other and yet oblivious to the true horrors which surrounded them.

She was frantic. Desperate to save her children. Unconcerned for her own fate.

Chapter Eight
Road to Bucha, Kyiv Oblast, Ukraine

The small band of Ukrainian troops turned on to a single lane road heading across farmland towards Bucha. They knew that they were getting close, and the Marines speed and determination only increased. They feared what they would find. But they were intent on getting there as fast as they could.

Ahead they heard the easily recognisable, sound of a tank, and the troops rapidly left the road and fanned out into the scrub setting themselves up in preparation for an ambush if the tank proved to be Russian.

They waited ten minutes before a T-80 and a small truck came into view. The tank was loaded on top with weary Russian soldiers. The Marines noted that the truck was also full of soldiers and another twenty or so infantrymen followed close behind on foot.

Marine Sergeant Marko Domitrovich silently signalled to two of his soldiers. They both carried NLAW anti-tank missiles. Within seconds they were ready to fire. Following orders, one took aim at the tank, and one aimed at the truck.

The first shot exploded the tank with a direct hit. The T-80s turret had blown off and men and metal exploded everywhere. The tank continued to explode as its shells ignited.

Suddenly the truck, which had just slewed to a halt, was also hit. The front of it had disappeared and the slaughter in the back of the truck was sheer carnage. None of the men had had body armour and the few who wore their helmets found that they gave them little protection. Many of the troops following the truck were injured or killed by flying debris and molten metal shards. Next the Ukrainians opened up with their rifles and light machine guns. Several petrified young Russians at the rear of the column managed to escape running back along the route that they had previously taken. The few who stayed did not live long. By the time the short skirmish was over most of the Russian troops were dead and the few who survived had terrible wounds which meant that most would not last the night.

The Marines briefly took a closer look and then head off. They had no time to tend to the wounded - they all wanted to get to Bucha without delay.

Chapter Nine
Road towards Kyiv, south of Bucha,
Kyiv Oblast, Ukraine

It was nearing noon when Kristina decided to take a chance and head for a nearby road. She knew that the children were flagging and that the going across country was far too slow. She felt that the Russian advance would pass them by if they were not careful. The road would increase their speed and they could possibly get a lift from a fellow, escaping Ukrainian.

Before stepping on to the road Kristina listened carefully and hearing nothing they stepped out and headed off. After twenty minutes they stopped as the children were completely exhausted. She broke a chocolate bar in half and gave each of them a piece. The children drank some water and then asked if they could pick some more wildflowers. Their mother knew that they had little will to go on, so she said that they could wait for five minutes. She kept listening for anything that would suggest danger. And then she heard it, but far too late.

The sound of a twig snapping signalled the arrival of the Russian patrol. Kristina turned suddenly and with a sharp intake of breath she saw a Russian private standing on the opposite side of the road having just emerge from the bushes. He was staring at her and had his rifle levelled at Kristina. Then more Russians appeared. They looked about nervously, and they also pointed their weapons directly at her. Eventually their Corporal emerged cautiously beside his soldiers. She looked in horror at his cruel smirk, thinking that she had never seen such a man, who looked almost half monster.

Corporal Koslov said in a slow lascivious drawl, 'Well, well! ... what have we got here!'

Kristina shivered with fear as the NCO slowly looked her up and down. She prayed that her children would remain hidden, but sadly they did not. The little boy appeared first from the nearby field with a handful of flowers for his mother. On seeing the soldiers, he ran to his mother and hugged her leg. Next his sister appeared, and she too went to her mother's side slipping her hand into her mother's open palm for comfort. The trembling fingers that gripped the child gave her no sense of comfort and she began to quietly weep.

Staring hard at Kristina, Corporal Koslov stepped forward and said, 'I'm going to have some fun with you, my pretty one!'

Suddenly, from among the men, Private Konstantin Orlov, marched out between the young family and Koslov. His weapon was levelled at the cruel Corporal as were his eyes. The men and Koslov looked stunned.

'We will let these people go!' the young man said with great determination.

'Is that so Orlov?' the NCO said in an ominous tone.

''They are civilians!' Konstantin said and half turned to the woman as he continued, 'Quickly, get going!'

The young mother said nervously,' Th …Thank you!'

She turned and began to walk away as fast as she could, looking over her shoulder as she did so.

Koslov's face softened and he said, 'Well done Orlov! I've made a soldier of you at last! You are right we do not have time to waste on her! Come on let's head off back to our own troops.'

He half turned and started walking towards the other soldiers as if they were going to make off in the other direction. The men looked at Koslov unbelievingly. They had come to know the man for what he was – the embodiment of pure evil. His actions, at that point, seemed so out of place that they were nonplussed.

Orlov dropped his weapon to his side as he stared happily at the Corporal who seemed to be heading back to his troops. The stream of bullets that hit the young man ripped through his stomach. Koslov had continued his turn making it swift and making it a full 360 degree. As he completed it his machine gun had risen to the horizontal and it was firing recklessly even before he could see Orlov again.

Suddenly, stunned, the Private fell to the ground in agony. A few paces behind him the mother and daughter lay lifeless in the dirt. Stray bullets from the stream that had been fired had ripped the life from them. The little boy stood alone beside the bodies his face outwardly showing his shock. He looked longingly at his lifeless mother and Sofia, his sister. Konstantin followed the angry gaze of the Corporal who looked at the dead woman. The private was incapable of stopping the Corporal as he pulled the trigger and killed the boy.

Little Grygoriy's body fell across his mothers and his hand dropped to the road still clutching his wreath of wildflowers.

Tears began to drop from Konstantin's eyes. Not tears of pain, but tears of sadness.

Koslov looked down at Orlov with a look of pure loathing. Then he stuck his boot firmly into the man's side. The Corporal suddenly turned to his men and said with venom, 'Throw this creature into the ditch so that he can die, slowly among the other rats!'

Chapter Ten
Road to Bucha, Kyiv Oblast, Ukraine

The Ukrainian Marines were on foot and were marching as fast as they could. They had returned to the road to speed up their advance, though they were concerned that it did leave them exposed. On hearing gunfire ahead, they had quickly dropped into the nearby ditch. Marko pulled a pair of binoculars from his pocket and scanned the area before them. He could see nothing untoward. In the distance a bend in the route ahead meant that he was unable to see everything.

The Sergeant signalled his troops to cross the road and to head through the neighbouring fields towards the sound of the gunfire. They tried to remain stealthy, but they were in haste. Coming closer to the unseen section of road they slowed their pace and crept slowly towards the drainage ditch which traced its path.

Chapter Eleven
Road to Bucha, Kyiv Oblast, Ukraine

The Russian soldiers ran forward to do the Corporals bidding. The brute then walked over to the dead woman looking down at her with disgust and dismay. Konstantin was roughly thrown into the ditch, unseen by the Corporal. As the brave young Russian desperately tried to cope with the pain, he saw his former comrades heading off to a nearby copse with the Corporal in tow.

They departed leaving Private Orlov in a crumpled heap. The boy soldier slipped his bloodied hand into his pocket and pulled out a small golden Russian Orthodox Cross from his pocket. The infantryman's mother had given the cross to him when he had joined the army. He was comforted by its familiar feel.

Momentarily, looking up at the sky he smiled to see the sun as it suddenly glimmered down on him. It had burst forth through a gap between two vast, white cumulus clouds whose shadows were slowly drifting across the landscape.

Brave Konstantin then began to pray before slipping briefly into unconsciousness.

Chapter Twelve
Road to Bucha, Kyiv Oblast, Ukraine

Seeing the civilians lying on the road one of the Ukrainian Marines went to investigate whilst his colleagues kept watch and provided cover. As the Marine crouched down to see if the mother and children were alive, he heard the pounding sound of running feet behind him.

His Sergeant had burst from the ditch and had run to the side of his family. He was followed by the rest of the troops who came forward with their guns at the ready.

Marko was distraught as he picked up the bodies of his children and held them to him as he stared through tear-filled eyes at his beloved wife. He could feel the still warm skin of his two children pressed hard against his face. The other troops were incredibly moved by their comrade's grief and the sight of his dead family. It also brought home thoughts of the Marines own families and their plight.

'Sergeant, I found one of them!' said a private who stood a few yards away half off the road. His eyes looked downwards indicating where the injured Russian lay.

Marko pulled the children from him and staring unbelievingly at them he laid them back beside their mother. He stared at them with a broken heart that would never mend. Then he closed his eyes and said a prayer for them.

He came up from his crouch and purposely walked over to the three soldiers who now surrounded the dying Russian.

'He is still alive Sergeant!' One of the soldiers whispered.

Sergeant Domitrovich pointed his weapon at the young Russians head.

'Sergeant! Wait! Wait!' the private who crouched beside the man said.

Then he continued, 'This boy says he tried to stop his NCO, a Corporal, from hurting your family. That is why the man shot them all! Apparently, the Russians have only just left. They have headed over towards those trees. He thinks they may be about to stop to eat.'

One of the other Marines said, 'It sounds like the truth. This man was shot in the chest and there is a separate pool of blood near your ...your family which was probably his. There is also a pile of spent shell casings over by the edge of the road on the other side. That must have been where the Corporal fired at them.'

Marko raised his head towards the small copse, and he began to march to it. Turning back to the group of Ukrainians who surrounded the Russian, Marko quietly said, 'Look after him!'

Marko strode fearlessly towards the point that the young Russian had mentioned. His eyes had filled with tears and his rage was indescribable.

One Marine waited with the dying soldier whilst the others went with their NCO. All of them were intent on retribution, but none more than Domitrovich.

The Marine who watched over the wounded infantryman noticed that he was slipping back into unconsciousness. He could hear the young man muttering almost incoherently to himself. It was a mixture of prayers and mention of his parents. The Ukrainian looked at the face that lay before him and wondered what had prompted the Russian soldier to stand up for the woman and children, when it would inevitably lead to his death at the hands of his own men.

Then the Marine gently stroked the infantryman's face and whispered to him, 'You are a good man!'

Chapter Thirteen
A Copse, near the Road to Bucha, Kyiv Oblast, Ukraine

The Russian Corporal was a lazy man. He was also scared. He had ordered his troops to light a fire and to get some food on. Koslov did not consider the necessity of placing sentries. It was a mistake that he would come to regret. The corporal's men began settling down for the night among the trees. They too were fearful, and they were completely exhausted. Each of them thought of Orlov and the little family. None particularly cared about their fate. However, they all wondered how quickly they could get away from their Corporal to prevent a similar outcome befalling them.

Koslov stood looking out at the fields ahead of his small party and wondering when he would be back in his beloved Moscow. Back to the safety of the barracks. The smoke effortlessly dribbled from his mouth as he lowered a cheap cigarette slowly to his side. Grinning, he thought to himself that he could spend the nights having drinks bought for him at a local bar while he told war stories to the drunken fools.

Nobody considered that the damp wood that they had foraged was creating more smoke than was wise amid a war zone. Smoke that could be seen for miles. But the eyes that watched the thin plume of smoke which rose high into the windless sky were not miles away. They were very close at hand. Close enough to clearly smell the smoke.

Most of the Russians were lying around sleeping or resting. The private who stoked the fire listened to the damp logs crack as the wood burnt. Koslov was the first to hear something out of place. It seemed distant at first, but it was not. It was the sound of running feet as they pounded into the wet ground.

Marko had no sense of fear as, on seeing the encampment, he had broken into a run with his machine gun levelled.

The flashes and noise from his weapon and those of his comrades who ran beside him violently woke the Russian soldiers from their slumber. The first to die was the man who tended the fire. He took a full burst in the chest as he had tried to turn and come up from his crouch. Hs lifeless body had fallen back into the hot embers.

The other Russian infantrymen panicked as they grabbed for their weapons, but the ferocity and suddenness of the Marines attack gave them no chance and most of them died before they even had a chance to fire a single shot. The cruel NCO who had stood a little further back amidst the trees watched motionless, horrified by the assault. He then turned and ran through the trees leaving his men to their fate. But he did not escape very far. Sergeant Marko had seen him, and he ran through the still dying Russian soldiers directly at Koslov firing a burst of lead into his legs. The cowards left kneecap had exploded with the only shot to hit him and he had fallen face down into the brush. He desperately tried to turn amidst his agony in a vain attempt to raise his weapon to defend himself. However, before he had the chance it was violently kicked from his hands by the Marine. Two of the brute's fingers had been broken in the attack and one of his knuckles was dislocated by the force.

Marko dropped his machine gun and the Russian half smiled in relief. But his respite disappeared once he saw the Marine draw a military knife with a serrated edge from its sheath which hung at his side from a camouflage belt. Seeing the look on the Ukrainian's face he let out a spine-tingling scream. It was to be the first of many, before he died.

The other Marines waited at the small encampment for Marko to return. They were all aware of the horrific sounds that had emanated from the bushes where their NCO had disappeared.

Marko retuned to them some time after everything had fallen silent. He was covered in blood and his face showed no emotion whatsoever. He did not speak, though they followed him back to the roadside.

On arriving they saw that the Marine that they had left behind was kneeling beside the young man from Saint Petersburg. The Sergeant crouched down beside him. The Russian boy, for that is what Marko saw in him, floated in and out of consciousness. When he was lucid, he would say prayers whilst clutching his Cross. He would repeatedly ask that they get the letters in his pocket to his mother and to tell her that he had died trying to save the little family. Marko promised that they would do as he asked. He held the young Russians hand and thanked him for what he had tried to do.

Moments later as Konstantin looked up at the passing clouds above, he smiled softly and went to his rest, gently fading into the next life. Though the Ukrainians hated the Russians for what they had done to their country, none of them could fail to be moved by the death of that young infantryman. Each of them prayed that there were more like him.

Marko took the letters from the dead soldiers' pockets and a photo of his mother from his wallet. Marko looked at the picture of the old woman who had a kindly smile.

He did not envy the person who had to tell her of the loss of her only son.

Her address was on the envelopes and the Church she went to was mentioned in the correspondence. The Sergeant would ensure that her son's wishes were fulfilled at the earliest point.

Then, with a heavy heart. he returned to his family and began to dig their graves with his entrenching tool, whilst his comrades buried the Russian soldier.

Chapter Fourteen
Chesme Church, Saint Petersburg, Russian Federation

Far away and in another country, an elderly Russian woman felt a dark cloud cross her soul. She had just left the cemetery and was heading on towards the church. Her steps had become heavier, and she began to feel a sickly sense of fear deep in her stomach.

Irina began climbing the steps of the ornate Orthodox Church as a sudden gust of wind brushed her face. She looked about and then, feeling fearful, she walked forward and pushed open the great, wooden door of the Church. The sudden warm, burst of air with its intense smell of incense rapidly calmed her. She went over and picked up a candle and thoughtfully lit it, staring deep into its flame before pressing it into position. Then she turned away and went to pray. The old woman found it so very hard to concentrate as she felt a terrible sense of doom that she could not shake.

Chapter Fifteen
The suburbs, Moscow, Russian Federation

The Marines finished their tour in Bucha and its surrounding area. The horrors they witnessed would affect them for ever. One of those men was later drafted into a secret regiment which was tasked with sabotage behind enemy lines. After receiving training in France with the Foreign Legion, he had made his way, with his team, to Moscow. They were there to set explosives off on railway lines in the suburbs.

Once their actions had begun to increase the level of security and subsequently their chance of detection, they moved their operations to Saint Petersburg. Before his team commenced their acts of sabotage in the new city, the former Marine headed off to one of the poorer residential districts. He waited in a nearby park and watched for the woman in the tattered old photo.

On seeing her leave her home he tailed her. The Ukrainian soldier intercepted her at the base of the steps to the Church. She was surprised and a little scared. He explained that he was a friend of her sons, and he then told her what had happened to him. The soldier also spoke of the young man's selfless bravery. He handed her the letters, the wooden Orthodox Cross, and a small case. The leather covered box held a medal for bravery with its accompanying citation which had been posthumously awarded to her son by the Ukrainian government. Tears ran down her face as she thanked the young man. Irina then squeezed his hand and looked furtively around.

She whispered knowingly, watching him through sad eyes, 'Your task is done, young man. Please leave now, it is not safe for you in this country.'

The saboteur smiled gently at the tearful woman and gave Irina a comforting hug. He could see where her son had gotten his humanity from.

Then he turned and sauntered over to a waiting car, glancing back at the poor old lady as he left. He thought to himself that she seemed to move more slowly and unsteadily as she climbed the steps towards the Church.

Irina looked back at the disappearing car and thought to herself, 'It is not safe for any of us anymore in Mother Russia!'

She lit a candle, read her sons letters, and had then prayed. As she came to the end of her prayers she felt at peace and her frail body gave up its last. The priest who found her, an hour later, lying on the floor noticed the Ukrainian medal in her hand and the small crucifix. Her still face looked serene and happy. Before anyone else arrived, he hid the items in his robes. Then he knelt and prayed for her.

Irina's funeral was attended by a few of the regular Churchgoers and was officiated over by the priest who had found her. It was a dull day and a light rain persistently fell from the sky. Before she was buried, he had asked for the coffin to be opened by the gravediggers. They thought it peculiar, but they did his bidding. Then the Orthodox priest placed the letters and the Cross in her hand. Unseen by anyone else, he slipped the Ukrainian medal into the coffin by her side, just before she was laid to rest with her beloved husband, Viktor. As the coffin was lowered into the rich, dark earth the clouds parted and the sun began to shine.

The few mourners all left, but the priest remained. He watched as the gravediggers methodically shovelled the soil on top of the coffin, as leaves danced about the gaping hole each time the wind blew. He had become weary of watching the poor parents who had all too frequently had to bury their sons, only to die themselves soon afterwards. They deserved better he thought. Then he said a final prayer for Irina, Viktor and their son and he turned and left, tracing his crooked path through the gravestones.

Chapter Sixteen
Azovstal Iron and Steel Works, Mariupol, Donetsk Oblast, Ukraine

Sergeant Marko Domitrovich eventually transferred to the Azov battalion. He had lost all will to live and he knew that the Azov would be in the very forefront of any battles. Shortly after he was transferred to Mariupol to join his new platoon. Marko fought heroically in Mariupol and was seen as a huge asset to his comrades. Under pressure from vastly superior numbers of Russians they slowly retreated into the vast warren of the Azovstal Iron and Steel Works. As the Russians closed in, the battle greatly intensified. It was a matter of national pride for Russia, to defeat and destroy the Azov battalion and to finally capture the ruins of the Azovstal.

The fighting was fierce. The Ukrainians were surrounded by Russians, their snipers, and the cream of their Special Forces. Every inch was fought over, and then fought over again as the slaughter continued.

The Ukrainians had secreted themselves among the warren of buildings, rubble, and tunnels. The battle continued relentlessly, and it was intense. And yet the besieged Ukrainian defenders continued to hold out. The world looked on in awe and sadness as they saw a modern-day Thermopylae play out before them. However, unlike the Spartans and their allies, the men and women did not die alone. Instead, they died in the full glare of the world media.

One evening during a particularly difficult firefight an incident had occurred which would propel Marko Domitrovich into legend.

A team of soldiers from a Russian Motor Rifle Brigade had been tasked with clearing out a large workshop which was mostly in ruins amid the Azovstal plant. They were brave and meticulous and though they had suffered incredible losses they were making headway. So much ordinance had been used that there was smoke and dust everywhere. Many of the Ukrainian defenders had been killed or wounded. Marko was pinned down in a foxhole amid the rubble with a female soldier called Larysa. A grenade landed near their hiding place and exploded almost instantly. Larysa fell back mortally wounded, her rifle still in her hand, having been hit in the neck and face by shrapnel. The Sergeant was also hit and momentarily stunned. He had been protected from the blast, in part, by the body of his comrade, though his face was badly lacerated by flying debris. Turning he saw the brave young woman, the life ebbing out of her.

At that point he also saw the image of his wife, in the face of the lifeless soldier, with the two dead children beside her. He lost all control and fear and ran from his foxhole like a madman. Racing over the undulating rubble he was not an easy target though the Russians kept firing at him and hitting him in the head and chest. But to their horror this demonic soldier with a blood red face and a look of madness kept coming on through the swirling smoke and mist, his machine gun firing volley after volley of supremely accurate shot at the Russians. Two Russian soldiers were shot and killed, and the apparition then turned and came running at the main group. Two more shots hit the apparition in the chest, but they did not stop him. At that, one petrified soldier broke and made a run for it to escape the Ukrainian ghost and then, they all ran. Several of them were killed as Marko continued coming on at them. When the attacking survivors had escaped, Marko fell to his knees utterly exhausted. There were some marks on his helmet from where bullets had ricocheted, but his camouflage tunic over his chest was totally shredded. He had been wearing an American bullet-proof vest under his outer jacket which had saved him. Moments later the roof caved in following a direct hit from a Russian artillery shell, finally entombing Marko.

Though he had been killed he had achieved mythic status among the Russian army! The men of the Motor Rifle Brigade spoke of the ghost soldier who could kill, but who could not be killed. They saw the clouds of dust rise up as the roof caved in, but it only further served to feed their belief. Many of them claimed to have seen strange shapes and evil faces among the dust clouds. Their officers tried to stop the rumours to prevent panic. However, when they next tried to get their men to fight and they themselves were clearly too scared to go with them, the legend had been born. It made the storming of the Azovstal immensely difficult for the besiegers.

Once the war was over the Ukrainian authorities intensified their efforts to find and bury their own dead and to return the Russian dead to their families.

In particular, the siege of the Azovstal had embedded itself on the collective psyche of the Ukrainian people. It came to embody the heroic bravery and the needless loss of life that they had suffered. No effort was spared to hunt through its ruins for those who had fallen within its walls. Of all the bodies of the soldiers that they searched for, one in particular was on the mind of all of the forensic teams, Sergeant Marko Domitrovich. Everyone knew his name and knew of his deeds which had drifted into myth.

Several weeks into their search and buried deep beneath rubble and twisted steel they eventually found him. The former Marine's body was carefully uncovered and identified, and a Ukrainian flag was respectfully lain over him. A captain from the Azov Regiment along with two representatives from the Marines who had watched over the search for their fallen compatriots then came to attention and saluted. As they did so, the captain quoted the ancient epitaph that had been penned centuries before by, Simonides of Ceos, 'Go tell the Spartans, stranger passing by, that here obedient to their laws we lie.'

It would later be determined that Domitrovich, had probably died from catastrophic injuries caused by shrapnel. But nobody believed it. Most people accepted that he had died from a broken heart.

Following a service in Bucha at the Ukrainian Orthodox church which he had attended as a boy, he was interred beside his family.

Chapter Seventeen
The Peace Shrine and Gravesite, on the road from Kyiv to Bucha, Kyiv Oblast, Ukraine

As the taxi driver recounted the story behind the strange event that she witnessed, the writer became deeply moved.

When Stepan had finished his tale, Amy looked about at the people who queued. Ukrainians, Belarussians, Georgians, British, French, Americans and Russians and many others were all quietly represented among their ranks. Some had come to pay their respects, some to atone, some to mourn, but all were there to give thanks for the peace that had been forged amid such a bitter conflict.

Amy thought of the horrors which Ukraine and its people had suffered. Hidden away, as it was, in the far east of Europe, she felt that she understood their wish to cling to something uplifting amid the carnage and the anguish.

The journalist waited in line with the driver. Eventually coming to the end of the queue she joined the throng who looked on at their quest. They were praying, crying, or thoughtfully staring. She gradually moved to the front and saw four graves. The father, Sergeant Marko Domitrovich, rested with his wife and his two little children. A few paces away she noted three other graves. Konstantin Orlov had been laid to rest near to where he too had fallen. Beside him were the graves of his beloved mother and father, Irina, and Viktor Orlov. After the war and at the request of the people of Ukraine, Konstantin's parents were exhumed, and they were laid to rest with their son in a lavish state funeral. Behind the graves a bronze stood on top of a stone plinth. It depicted a brave young Russian soldier in his dying moments as he desperately tried to shield a Ukrainian mother and her two young children.

Carved deep into the plinth was an ancient inscription by Vergil, 'Omnia Vincit Amor et nos cedamus amori' - 'Love conquers all; let us all yield to love.'

The arm of the Russian soldier shone brightly in the sunshine as it was constantly touched or patted by the passers-by as they left. It had become commonplace, and nobody really knew why or when it had started. Some thought that it was for luck, others as a mark of respect.

Wildflowers stretched as far as the eye could see, deep into the shallow valley which fell away from the road.

Amy watched people pass by the graves as they tapped each one with flowers, their hand, or bags of seeds. She noticed an elderly Russian couple who were both weeping. The wife inadvertently dropped some bags of seeds and Amy picked them up. Amy returned the seeds to the woman who continued to weep. The elderly lady smiled and thanked her profusely in Russian. Then she gave the journalist one packet of seeds back and squeezed Amy's hand. The reporter's eyes welled up as she thanked the woman. She watched the Russian couple as they left and then Amy went over to the bronze and touched it as everyone else did. She could not explain why, but she felt at that moment as if the experience was electrifying.

Looking back at the graves Amy noticed that Marko and Konstantin both had the image of the Hero of Ukraine chiselled into their gravestones. They had received the medals posthumously.

Amy walked a respectful distance away into the nearby field and then she crouched down. Taking out her pen and notebook she began to write. There were smudges in places on the paper as tears fell from her face.

On the journey back to Kyiv, Amy asked Stepan to stop on the side of the road, just as she had seen many others do. The reporter took the bag from her pocket and sprinkled the wildflower seeds about her.

Epilogue
Chicago Tribune Headquarters, Freedom Center, Chicago, Illinois, USA

Amy sat at a long, oak table looking out wistfully at the great city stretching far into the distance. She had been in the Chicago Tribune's headquarters before, but Amy had never met the legendary Editor-in-Chief, Mitch Pugh.

She should have been excited, but her time in Ukraine and the story the freelancer had written had exerted a profound change in her.

Mitch had noticed the distant look in the young reporter's eyes. He had seen it before in other reporters, of course. Those brave people often risked their lives to give a voice to the oppressed and the friendless.

'But at what personal cost?' He pondered.

As he studied Amy's face he wondered if the horrors she had seen and the story the young woman had written of, had come at too high a price?

Pugh said kindly, 'Well Amy, your series of articles on Ukraine has been a huge success!'

She said nothing for a few seconds before replying, 'Yes ...I suppose it has been.'

Thoughtful, she continued, 'Someone had to write of their terrible story.'

'Yes indeed.' Pugh responded.

Then he continued in a soft and collaborative tone, 'Look Amy. We were all very impressed with what you have done. I want you to join the team permanently. You will have a free reign as to what you chose to write about. What do you say? It would be great to have you on board.'

She turned to the Editor-in-Chief who was making a most generous offer and one which she could not have even dreamed of before. But Amy was weary. What she had experienced in Ukraine and the stories she had heard had taken their toll. They had also made her re-assess her life and her future.

The young reporter sighed heavily, smiled softly, and said, 'Thank you for your offer. It is a real privilege to receive it. But ...I'm sorry. I will have to decline.'

Pugh knew that any journalist would have chewed his arm off for such an offer. But he was experienced in reading faces, and he knew that nothing he could say would alter her decision.

He thought for a moment and then said, 'Yes, I feared that you would say that!'

Then he continued, 'May I ask what you will do now?'

Her face visibly brightened as she quipped, 'Well! ... I'm going to head to the Argentine.'

'Wow! What will you do there?'

Her mouth opened in the brightest of smiles showcasing her gleaming white teeth, 'Nothing ...I'm going to do absolutely nothing ...except drink and eat and explore!'

Pugh grinned and said, 'I hear they have the greatest steaks down there and fine wines too. Maybe if you get bored you could scribble a few lines about your experiences in the southern hemisphere for our readers!'

Amy looked thoughtful and said, 'Thank you, Yes, maybe I will just pack a pencil and some paper along with my Fodors' travel guide.'

Two days later a young woman sat in the departure lounge at Chicago O'Hare International Airport waiting for her flight and looking forward to her eventual location, Buenos Aires.

Becoming fidgety, she pulled a pencil and a notebook from her backpack, stared at the blank page and after a brief pause, thought again of the generous offer from the Editor-in-Chief. She sighed heavily and ...relieved, she wrote a title '...With Love from the Argentine!'

Thinking again she scribbled a sub-title, 'Chimichurri – what's not to know and love!'

And then she began to write ...

AFTERWORD

Thank you for taking the time to read or listen my book. I hope that you enjoyed it.

You can greatly help me and potential new readers by leaving a review. As long or as short a review as you wish would be great.

I read all reviews and greatly appreciate the time and effort that my readers go to in leaving them.

If you wish to join my mailing list to be among the first to hear about forthcoming books and deals, then please sign up at: **www.idograf.com**

Thank you.

Ido Graf

About the Author

Ido Graf grew up in the Mediterranean and in the United Kingdom, predominantly in London.

After studying for a bachelor's degree, Ido went on to study for a masters, before taking other specialist qualifications.

He spent some time in military bases in Europe and the Middle East and comes from a police & military background.

Ido has travelled extensively in North & South America, Europe, Africa, the Far East, Russia, and the former Eastern bloc countries.

He was questioned at length in Guinea by the Presidential Guard on spying allegations relating to the

Presidential Palace and in Sierra Leone by agents of the state concerning alleged diamond smuggling.

Ido and a friend of his once engaged in a shooting competition in the Củ Chi district of Ho Chi Minh City, with John F. Kennedy while Jr. Daryl Hannah watched the three of them as they fired AK-47s. It was an extraordinary, chance encounter when they were travelling in Vietnam in the 1990s.

Ido is a fully qualified scuba diver and skydiver. He is a proficient snowboarder, skier (both downhill and cross-country) and a highly experienced alpinist.

He has worked in various sectors for both government departments and private concerns in a variety of sensitive fields in the UK and North America.

Ido Graf is a writer of mystery and suspense thrillers. His works, which he is now publishing, are derived from his own experiences and from meticulous research. He visits all of the locations that he writes about to maintain the highest standards of realism within his novels.

Though much of his output is contemporary in nature, it frequently has a historical basis at its core.

The focus of his books is in the political, corporate espionage, thriller, and adventure categories.

He hopes that you enjoy his novels. Please follow Ido Graf on his blog:

https://www.idograf.com

Acknowledgements

Each of these people or groups have had an impact on my writing and on my will to write.

On some occasions, they may have felt that their contribution was minimal, but their impact was tremendous and at some moments, crucial.

Special thanks for their support, critical appraisal, guidance, and encouragement:

Family and friends including

My darling wife and my sons

Andy, Mark, David & Kerri, Ian, K.W.,

Gerlinde

John & Tammy

Paul & Gwyneth

Inspirations

The many authors of fiction which I have read including, among others, such greats as Graham Greene, John le Carré, Frederick Forsyth, Nelson DeMille, Robert Harris, John Grisham, Jack Higgins, Mark Dawson, Thomas Hardy, Evelyn Waugh, Desmond Bagley, Hammond Innes, Helen MacInnes, Alistair MacLean, Robert Wilson, Randy Wayne White
and most of all the works and inspiring life journey of Lee Child.

The kindness, encouragement and tutoring of novelists: Frederick E. Smith and Rosemary Aitken.

Also

Special thanks go to those people, some I may never even have known or met, throughout my life who have extended to me - kindness, support, and assistance even though, on occasion, there was no reason to have expected it.

Any successes in my writing are built on the shoulders of those mentioned above, any faults are solely my own.